Daily Encounters With God

A 30-DAY DEVOTIONAL

Co-Pastor Cynthia Brown

Each day presents a carefully selected Scripture passage designed to inspire you and guide your reflection. Next to this passage, you will find a short Encounter Word that captures the main idea and encourages you to connect with its meaning on a personal level. Each entry also includes a heartfelt Prayer to express gratitude, seek guidance, and promote inner peace. Finally, you will find an actionable response to help you apply these teachings in your daily life.

Daily Encounters With God – A 30-Day Devotional

ISBN: 979-8-9926902-8-6

Published by: Harrod Publisher

Unless otherwise noted, all scriptural citations in this book come from the King James (KJV) Version of the Bible.

Printed in the United States of America.

About

Each day presents a carefully selected Scripture passage designed to inspire you and guide your reflection. Next to this passage, you will find a short Encounter Word that captures the main idea and encourages you to connect with its meaning on a personal level. Each entry also includes a heartfelt Prayer to express gratitude, seek guidance, and promote inner peace. Finally, you will find an actionable response to help you apply these teachings in your daily life.

Acknowledgement

I give heartfelt thanks and honor to my amazing husband, Bishop Ronald Brown, Sr., my children, and my grandchildren, who are the greatest joy of my life!

Table of Contents

Day 1

The God Who Comes Near

Scripture: *James 4:8 — "Draw near to God and He will draw near to you."*

Reflection: God is not distant. Your journey toward a deeper relationship with Him begins with the conscious decision to draw near. He is eagerly waiting for you to seek Him, invite Him into your daily life, and ask for His assistance, wisdom, and guidance. When we actively seek God in every decision we face, we cultivate a reliance on Him that transforms our approach to all areas of our lives. This practice nurtures our spiritual growth and strengthens our faith.

Prayer: Lord, I come to you today because I need and depend on you. Please meet me at this moment; I seek your help, wisdom, and guidance. I do not want to move forward without your presence. Surround me with your love and light as I navigate my path today.

My Reflection:

Day 2

Expect The Unexpected

Scripture: *Exodus 3:2 — "The bush was on fire, but it did not burn up."*

Reflection: Encounters with God often happen in surprising ways. It is essential to remain alert to the supernatural elements that may appear in our everyday lives. Expect God to reveal Himself in unexpected moments, and trust that He will move on our behalf in ways only He can. Allow Him to demonstrate His power in your life and be open to the miraculous that can unfold at any time. This awareness can lead to profound experiences that enrich our faith journey.

Prayer: Father, help me notice You in the unusual and unexpected moments of my life. When I find myself struggling and uncertain about my future, and especially when I am least expecting you, please show up for me and release your power. I trust that you are always present, even in the chaos.

My Reflection:

Day 3

Holy Ground

Scripture: *Exodus 3:5 — "Take off your sandals, for the place where you are standing is holy ground."*

Reflection: God's presence sanctifies space. Are you treating your environment as holy today? Recognizing the sacredness of where we stand can change our perspective and help us approach our surroundings with reverence. When we honor the places, we occupy as holy, we invite God's presence to dwell within them and transform our experiences. This mindset encourages us to seek His presence in all places, recognizing that every moment can be an encounter with the divine.

Prayer: Lord, make my heart and environment holy for You. Sanctify every area of my life, from my thoughts and actions to my surroundings. Help me to see Your presence in every corner of my life and to honor You with all that I am.

My Reflection:

Day 4

Called by Name

Scripture: *Isaiah 43:1 — "I have called you by name; you are mine."*

Reflection: God knows you personally. You are not merely a statistic or a number; you are His beloved. This intimate relationship brings a sense of belonging and purpose that is unparalleled. Understanding that God calls you by name reinforces the idea that you are valued and cherished. This personal connection can provide comfort and strength as you navigate life's challenges, knowing that you are never alone.

Prayer: Jesus, thank You for knowing me and for calling me by name. I am grateful to understand that I belong to You and that I am loved beyond measure. Help me to embrace my identity in You and to walk confidently in my purpose.

My Reflection:

____

____

____

Day 5

Encounter in The Secret Place

Scripture: *Matthew 6:6 — "Go into your room... your Father who sees in secret will reward you."*

Reflection: Make space for God in your life. He shows up where He is invited and where there is intentionality. Creating a secret place for prayer and reflection allows you to cultivate a deeper intimacy with the Lord. It is in these quiet moments that you can hear His voice more clearly and receive His guidance. When you prioritize time with God, you open the door for transformative encounters that enrich your spiritual journey.

Prayer: I welcome You, Lord, into the secret places of my life. I invite You into every area of my existence, from my thoughts to my actions. May I always seek to create a space for You, knowing that Your presence brings peace and understanding.

My Reflection:

Day 6

When God Whispers

Scripture: *1 Kings 19:12 — "After the fire came a gentle whisper."*

Reflection: God often speaks softly rather than loudly. In the midst of our busy lives, silence can be a powerful tool that helps us hear His gentle whispers. Taking time to quiet our minds and hearts allows us to tune into the voice of the Spirit. It is in this stillness that we can find clarity and direction, as we learn to discern His voice amidst the noise of the world. Cultivating this habit can deepen our relationship with God and enhance our spiritual awareness.

Prayer: Tune my ears to the whisper of Your Spirit. Help me to hear You when You speak to me, amidst the distractions and chaos of life. Teach me to embrace the silence, for it is in that space that I can truly connect with You.

My Reflection:

Day 7

Was That You, Lord?

Scripture: *1 Samuel 3:10 — "Speak, for your servant is listening."*

Reflection: Learning to recognize God's voice comes with practice and intentionality. It requires us to be attentive and open to His guidance in our daily lives. As we cultivate a relationship with Him, we begin to discern the subtle nudges and promptings that come from His Spirit. This process of spiritual growth is essential for aligning our lives with His will. Over time, we become more attuned to His voice, allowing it to guide our decisions and actions.

Prayer: Speak to me, Lord. I'm listening for Your voice, and I want to know You more intimately. Help me to be sensitive to Your leading and to follow where You guide.

My Reflection:

____

____

____

Day 9

The Power of His Presence

Scripture: *Psalm 16:11 — "In Your presence there is fullness of joy."*

Reflection: Time spent in God's presence refreshes and revives our spirits. It is in His presence that we find true joy and fulfillment, regardless of our circumstances. When we intentionally seek Him, we invite His peace and comfort into our lives. This connection not only uplifts us but also empowers us to face challenges with a renewed perspective. Embracing His presence can transform our hearts and minds, leading to a deeper understanding of His love and grace.

Prayer: Fill me with joy today as I dwell with You. You are my Peace, and I long to experience the fullness of Your presence. May Your joy overflow in my life and impact those around me as well.

My Reflection:

____

____

____

Day 9

The Fear of The Lord

Scripture: *Proverbs 9:10 — "The fear of the Lord is the beginning of wisdom."*

Reflection: Reverence brings revelation. When we honor God's holiness and recognize His greatness, we begin to gain true wisdom. This understanding allows us to navigate life with discernment and clarity. A healthy fear of the Lord leads to a deeper relationship with Him, where we are open to His teachings and corrections. Through this reverence, we discover the profound truths of His word and the ways He desires to guide us.

Prayer: Lord, teach me to walk in reverence before You. Help me to honor You in my thoughts, words, and actions. May my life reflect the wisdom that comes from a deep and respectful relationship with You.

My Reflection:

____

____

____

Day 10

Glory Encounters

Scripture: *2 Corinthians 3:18 — "We are being transformed... into His image."*

Reflection: When you behold Him, you begin to become like Him. Our encounters with God's glory have the power to transform us from the inside out. As we seek Him and experience His presence, we are shaped into His likeness, reflecting His character in our lives. This transformation is not merely external but impacts our thoughts, actions, and relationships. By embracing these glory encounters, we open ourselves to a life that mirrors His love and grace.

Prayer: Transform me as I behold Your glory. Help me to reflect Your image in all that I do, so that others may see Your light shining through me. May my life be a testament to Your love and truth.

My Reflection:

____

____

____

Day 11

Faith Awakens Encounter

Scripture: *Hebrews 11:6 — "He rewards those who earnestly seek Him."*

Reflection: Faith is the key that opens the door to encounter. When we earnestly seek God with a sincere heart, we position ourselves to experience His presence in profound ways. This pursuit of faith not only deepens our understanding of who He is but also enriches our relationship with Him. As we step out in faith, we unlock the rewards of knowing Him intimately and experiencing His goodness. Faith empowers us to embrace the extraordinary encounters that shape our lives.

Prayer: believe You're near, and I seek You now. Open my eyes to see You and my heart to receive what You have for me. May my faith lead me to transformative encounters with You.

My Reflection:

____

____

____

Day 12

Come Up Higher

Scripture: *Revelation 4:1 — "Come up here, andI will show you..."*

Reflection: God invites you to go deeper, higher, and further in your relationship with Him. This call to ascend is an invitation to experience greater revelations of His strength, power, and glory. When we respond to this invitation, we open ourselves to new dimensions of understanding and connection with the divine. It is a journey that challenges us to leave behind the familiar and embrace the unknown with faith. Each step upward brings us closer to His heart and to the purpose of our lives.

Prayer: Take me higher in You, Lord. Show me, reveal to me Your strength, Your power, and Your glory! I am ready to embrace the depths of Your presence and the heights of Your love.

My Reflection:

Day 13

The Fire of God

Scripture: *Hebrews 12:29 — "Our God is a consuming fire."*

Reflection: God's fire purifies and ignites passion within us. This consuming fire is not meant to destroy but to refine our hearts and souls. As we encounter His fire, we are cleansed of impurities and empowered to live fervently for Him. This transformation can ignite a deep passion for His purposes, driving us to share His love with others. Embracing the fire of God can lead to a life filled with purpose, passion, and a desire to reflect His light in the world.

Prayer: Burn away what doesn't please You. Purify my heart and ignite my spirit with a passion for Your ways. May I be a vessel of Your love and grace, shining brightly in a world that needs You.

My Reflection:

___

___

___

Day 14

The Encounter That Changes Everything

Scripture: *Acts 9:3–6 — Paul's Damascus encounter.*

Reflection: One encounter with God can shift your destiny. Paul's dramatic transformation on the road to Damascus serves as a powerful reminder of the life-altering impact of divine encounters. When we open ourselves to the possibility of encountering God, we position ourselves for radical change and new beginnings. These moments can redefine our purpose and redirect our lives in extraordinary ways. Embracing such encounters invites God to work miracles in our hearts and futures. Prayer:

Change me, Lord, with one touch from You. I am open to Your transformative power, ready to embrace the new life You have for me. Let me be forever changed by Your love and grace.

My Reflection:

____

____

____

Day 15

Stay With Him

Scripture: *John 15:4 — "Remain in me, and I will remain in you."*

Reflection: Don't just visit God—abide in Him. The invitation to remain in His presence is a call to cultivate a deep, lasting relationship with the Father. This abiding presence sustains us and empowers us to live out our faith daily. When we choose to stay connected to Him, we draw strength, wisdom, and peace that surpasses all understanding. This relationship is not meant to be transactional but transformational, leading us to a life that reflects His love.

Prayer: Help me live in Your presence daily. Teach me how to abide deeply in You, so that my life may overflow with Your love and grace. I long to remain in You as You remain in me.

My Reflection:

____

____

____

Day 16

The Weight of His Glory

Scripture: *Isaiah 6:1 — "I saw the Lord... high and lifted up."*

Reflection: God's glory humbles us and brings clarity to our lives. When we encounter His greatness, we are reminded of our place in the grand scheme of creation. This humility fosters a deeper understanding of who we are and leads us to seek His wisdom and guidance in our lives. Witnessing His glory can shift our focus from ourselves to His purpose, allowing us to live with intention and gratitude. It is in recognizing His glory that we find true clarity and direction.

Prayer: Reveal Your glory to me today. Like You did for the prophet Isaiah, show me Your splendor and majesty. May this encounter transform my heart and mind, aligning me with Your will.

My Reflection:

____

____

____

Day 17

He Still Speaks

Scripture: *John 10:27 — "My sheep hear my voice."*

Reflection: God still speaks to those who follow Him. His voice is a guiding light in our lives, leading us toward His plans and purposes. As His sheep, we are called to cultivate a relationship that allows us to recognize and respond to His guidance. This requires intentional listening and a willingness to obey. By prioritizing our connection with Him, we can be assured that He is actively communicating with us each day.

Prayer: I'm Your sheep, and I'm listening. Help me to discern Your voice amidst the noise of the world. May I be attentive to Your leading and eager to follow where You guide.

My Reflection:

Day 18

Encounter Brings Identity

Scripture: *Judges 6:12 — "The Lord is with you, mighty warrior."*

Reflection: God calls you to be who you are becoming. This powerful affirmation invites us to see ourselves through His eyes, recognizing our potential and purpose. Understanding our identity in Him allows us to embrace the journey of becoming who He has destined us to be. This process involves growth, transformation, and the realization that we are not defined by our past but rather by His promises. Embracing this identity empowers us to live boldly and faithfully.

Prayer: Help me see myself as You see me. May I embrace my identity as Your beloved child, equipped and empowered to fulfill Your purpose. Guide me in my journey of becoming all that You intend for me.

My Reflection:

____

____

____

Day 19

The Silence of God

Scripture: *Psalm 46:10 — "Be still and know that I am God."*

Reflection: Silence isn't absence; it's an invitation to deeper intimacy with God. In the stillness, we can encounter His presence and hear His voice more clearly. This quiet time is essential for developing trust and understanding in our relationship with Him. Learning to be still allows us to reflect, pray, and listen, creating space for God to reveal Himself in profound ways. Embracing the silence as a sacred time can lead to greater clarity and connection.

Prayer: Teach me to be still and trust You. Help me embrace the silence as an opportunity to connect with You more deeply. May I find comfort and strength in Your presence during these quiet moments.

My Reflection:

___

___

___

Day 20

Wrestling For The Blessing

Scripture: *Genesis 32:26 — "I will not let you go unless You bless me."*

Reflection: Sometimes, encounters with God require persistence and determination. Just as Jacob wrestled with the angel for his blessing, we too are called to seek God earnestly and relentlessly. This wrestling can lead to profound encounters that transform our lives and deepen our faith. Persistence in prayer and pursuit of God's presence can result in blessings that redefine our circumstances and align us with His purpose. Embracing this struggle can lead to a deeper understanding of His character and promises.

Prayer: I won't let go until You bless me. Grant me the strength and determination to pursue You with all my heart. May my persistence lead to encounters that change my life and deepen my relationship with You.

My Reflection:

____

____

____

Day 21

Encounter in Surrender

Scripture: *Romans 12:1 — "Offer your bodies as a living sacrifice."*

Reflection: God meets us where we surrender our will and desires to Him. This act of offering ourselves as living sacrifices opens the door for divine encounters. Surrendering allows us to let go of our control and trust in His perfect plan. In this space of submission, we can experience His transformative power and align our lives with His purpose. Embracing surrender as a pathway to encounter can lead to profound spiritual growth and deeper intimacy with God.

Prayer: I lay my life before You today. Help me to truly surrender all that I am to You, trusting that Your plans are greater than my own. May each act of surrender lead to deeper encounters with Your love and grace.

My Reflection:

____

____

____

Day 22

Divine Interruptions

Scripture: *Luke 1:26–38 — Mary's angelic encounter.*

Reflection: God's plans often interrupt our own—always for the better. Mary's encounter with the angel Gabriel serves as a powerful reminder of how divine interruptions can lead to extraordinary outcomes. When we remain open to these interruptions, we allow God to work in our lives in ways we may not have anticipated. Embracing these moments can lead to growth, learning, and the fulfillment of His promises. Trusting in His timing and purpose can transform our understanding of our circumstances.

Prayer: Let it be unto me according to Your word. Help me to trust in Your divine interruptions and to embrace the new paths You are leading me on. May I be open to the plans You have for my life, knowing they are always for my good.

My Reflection:

Day 23

Prepare Him Room

Scripture: *Luke 3:4 — "Prepare the way for the Lord."*

Reflection: Clear space in your heart and schedule for God. Preparing Him room in our lives allows us to focus on what truly matters and to prioritize our relationship with Him. This intentionality creates opportunities for encounters that can transform our hearts and minds. As we create space for God, we position ourselves to receive His guidance, blessings, and love. Making room for Him requires us to let go of distractions and embrace the divine moments He offers.

Prayer: I make room for You today. Help me to clear my heart and schedule, allowing Your presence to fill every part of my life. I desire to prioritize You above all else and welcome Your guidance and love.

My Reflection:

Day 24

The Cloud and The Fire

Scripture: *Exodus 13:21 — God led them by cloud and fire.*

Reflection: God guides us through His presence, just as He led the Israelites by cloud and fire in the wilderness. This imagery serves as a powerful reminder of His constant guidance and protection. When we seek His presence, we can trust that He will lead us through life's challenges and uncertainties. Recognizing His guidance can provide comfort and direction as we navigate our journeys. By staying attuned to His leading, we can experience the fullness of His plans for our lives.

Prayer: Lead me, Lord, by Your Spirit. Help me to be sensitive to Your guidance and to follow where You lead. May I trust in Your presence to navigate the path ahead.

My Reflection:

____

____

____

Day 25

Face to Face

Scripture: *Exodus 33:11 — "The Lord would speak to Moses face to face."*

Reflection: Intimacy with God is available to those who actively pursue it. The relationship Moses had with God, speaking face to face, illustrates the depth of connection we can have with our Creator. When we seek Him earnestly, we can experience profound moments of closeness and understanding. This pursuit of intimacy invites us to engage in deeper conversations with God, allowing us to know Him more fully. Striving for this connection can lead to transformative encounters that shape our spiritual lives.

Prayer: I want to know You face to face. Help me to pursue intimacy with You in every aspect of my life. May our relationship deepen, and may I experience the fullness of Your love and grace.

My Reflection:

____

____

____

Day 26

Stay Hungry

Scripture: *Matthew 5:6 — "Blessed are those who hunger..."*

Reflection: Staying spiritually hungry and thirsty for God's presence and truth is essential for growth. When we long for more of Him, we open our hearts to receive His blessings and revelations. This hunger drives us to seek Him through prayer, worship, and the study of His word. Cultivating a desire for God encourages us to explore the depths of His love and grace, leading us to a more fulfilling spiritual journey. Embracing this hunger can transform our lives and inspire those around us.

Prayer: I desire to stay hungry for You, Lord. Help me to seek You earnestly and to cultivate a heart that longs for Your presence. May my spiritual hunger lead me to deeper encounters with You.

My Reflection:

___

___

___

Day 27

Revival Begins With Me

Revival is not simply a series of events or gatherings; it originates within the hearts of individuals who earnestly seek a deeper relationship with God. True revival manifests when people recognize their need for humility and turn toward God with sincerity. It is a movement that begins in the personal lives of believers, igniting passion and commitment to spiritual growth. When a heart is genuinely hungry for the presence of God, it becomes a catalyst for transformation, not just within oneself but also in the community. Each individual has the power to initiate a ripple effect of revival, demonstrating that change starts with a personal encounter with the divine.

In prayer, we express our desire for revival, inviting God to stir within us a longing for His presence. It is a heartfelt plea for transformation that starts internally but extends outwardly to touch others. By asking for revival to begin in us, we commit to being vessels of His love and grace. This prayer is a powerful declaration of our intention to be agents of change, fostering an atmosphere where God's spirit can move freely. As we seek Him earnestly, we become more attuned to His voice and guidance, leading to profound spiritual awakening.

The journey of revival requires reflection on our hearts and lives, and an assessment of where we stand in our relationship with God. It calls for a willingness to confront areas that need change and to surrender those aspects to Him.

This introspection can be challenging, yet it is essential for true transformation to take place. By recognizing our shortcomings and weaknesses, we create space for God's strength to manifest in our lives. Ultimately, revival is a process that fosters renewal and deepens our connection with the Lord.

As individuals encounter revival, the impact resonates within their communities, inspiring others to seek the same transformative experience. The collective hunger for God's presence can lead to powerful movements that change the spiritual landscape of entire regions. When people come together with a shared longing for revival, they can create an environment where God's work isevident and lives are transformed. This communal pursuit not only strengthens the faith of individuals but also promotes growth and unity within the body of Christ. The revival that begins in one heart can indeed spark a movement that reaches far beyond what any individual could achieve alone.

To see revival take root, there must be a commitment to action and faith. It requires stepping out of comfort zones, engaging in acts of service, and being willing to share the gospel message. This commitment to living out one's faith is essential in fostering an environment where revival can flourish. As we act on our prayers and seek God's guidance, we must be prepared to embrace the changes He brings into our lives. Revival is not just a moment in time; it is a continuous journey of faith that invites us to grow deeper in our relationship with Him.

My Reflection:

____

____

____

Day 28

The Anointing to Go

Anointing is a divine empowerment that equips believers for their kingdom assignments. According to Isaiah 61:1, the Spirit of the Lord empowers individuals to fulfill their purpose and calling. This anointing is not simply for personal benefit; it is intended to be shared with others as we engage in service and ministry. When we recognize the anointing on our lives, we understand that we are called to be conduits of God's grace and love in a world that desperately needs it. Embracing this empowerment invites us to step boldly into the mission He has for us.

Each encounter with God can lead to a greater understanding of our unique calling within the body of Christ. The anointing to go is a reminder that we are not meant to be passive recipients of His grace but active participants in spreading His message. This calling may manifest in various forms, whether through teaching, serving, or simply sharing our testimonies with those around us. It is crucial to recognize that our assignments are divinely orchestrated and that we have the tools necessary to fulfill them. By acknowledging our purpose, we can walk confidently in the anointing that empowers us.

The process of being anointed for action often requires spiritual growth and preparation. We must be willing to submit to God’s leading, allowing Him to shape us into the vessels He desires us to be. This growth involves spending time in His Word, engaging in prayer, and surrounding ourselves with a community of believers who encourage us. Aswe grow spiritually, we become more attuned to the Holy

Spirit's promptings, enabling us to respond effectively to His call. Ultimately, our empowerment is rooted in our relationship with God, which fuels our passion for service.

Stepping out in faith to fulfill our anointed mission often requires courage. It can be daunting to share our faith or serve in unfamiliar settings, but God equips us with the strength we need. The anointing gives us the assurance that we are not alone in our endeavors; He walks with us every step of the way.

As we act on our faith, we witness the transformative power of God at work in our lives and the lives of others. This journey of service becomes a testament to His faithfulness and love, inspiring others to seek their own anointing for action.

Our anointing to go is ultimately about making a lasting impact for the Kingdom of God. It calls us to engage in acts of service that reflect His heart for humanity. As we respond to this anointing, we contribute to the advancement of His Kingdom on Earth, bringing hope and healing to those who encounter us. Each act of service, no matter how small, is significant in the grand narrative of God's redemptive plan. By embracing our anointing, we become part of a larger movement that seeks to bring glory to God and transform lives.

My Reflection:

____

____

____

Day 29

Guard The Encounter

It is vital to protect the intimate encounters we have with God, as these moments often shape our spiritual journey. Proverbs 4:23 emphasizes the importance of guarding our hearts, for they are the wellspring of life. When we experience a profound encounter with the Lord, we gain insights and revelations that can deeply impact our faith. However, such experiences can be vulnerable, making it essential to safeguard them from distractions and negativity. By diligently guarding our hearts, we ensure that the intimacy we've gained remains intact and continues to bear fruit.

The revelations we receive during our encounters with God are precious and should be treated with care. These insights not only enrich our personal relationship with Him but also provide guidance for our daily lives. It is crucial to protect these revelations from doubt, fear, or criticism that can arise from external sources. By nurturing the intimacy we've built with God, we allow these insights to flourish and guide our decisions. This protective stance fosters a deeper connection with Him, enabling us to experience more profound encounters in the future.

Guarding our encounters requires discernment and focus, as we must identify what influences we allow into our hearts and minds. We should be mindful of the messages we consume, whether from media, conversations, or our own thoughts. Keeping our focus on God and His promises helps us to maintain the clarity needed to protect our spiritual encounters. Engaging in practices such as prayer, worship, and meditation can strengthen our resolve to guard our hearts. By doing so, we cultivate an environment conducive to ongoing encounters with Him.

Protecting the encounters we have with God is also a matter of stewardship. We are entrusted with the revelations He gives us, and it is our responsibility to nurture and grow them. This commitment requires faithfulness to stay connected to Him and to actively seek His presence in our lives. As we faithfully guard our encounters, we demonstrate our gratitude for the intimacy He provides. This stewardship establishes a foundation for future encounters, where we can continue to grow in our relationship with Him.

Every time we guard our encounters, we set the stage for transformation and growth in our spiritual lives. These moments remind us of God's faithfulness and His unwavering desire for a relationship with us. As we prioritize the protection of our intimate experiences with Him, we open ourselves up to continual renewal and understanding. This commitment to guarding our encounters ultimately leads to a deeper, more transformative walk of faith. By cherishing and safeguarding these experiences, we create a legacy of faith that can influence others.

My Reflection:

____

____

____

Day 30

Invitation to Ongoing Encounter

Revelation 3:20 presents a powerful image of God's invitation to engage with Him daily. This scripture portrays God standing at the door, patiently knocking and waiting for us to respond. His invitation is not a one-time event but an ongoing opportunity to experience His presence in ourlives. Each day offers a fresh chance to open our hearts and minds to His calling, inviting Him into the depths of our being. By recognizing this invitation, we can cultivate a lifestyle of continual encounters with the Lord.

Welcoming God into our lives is a profound act of faith and surrender. It signifies our desire for Him to dwell within us, guiding our actions and shaping our thoughts. As we invite the Lord into our daily routines, we create a sacred space where He can reveal Himself more fully. This act of welcoming Him is not just about seeking His presence during times of need; it is an acknowledgment of His constant desire to be involved in every aspect of our lives. By making our lives a place He loves to dwell, we foster a deeper relationship with Him.

The invitation to ongoing encounters requires our engagement and commitment to pursue Him intentionally. It is essential to carve out time for prayer, worship, and reflection to ensure we remain connected to Him. This commitment can take various forms, from quiet moments of solitude to engaging in community worship. As we prioritize these encounters, we find that our relationship with God flourishes, leading to a richer spiritual life. Our willingness to engage with Him opens the door to deeper insights and revelations.

Being open to God's presence means being receptive to the ways He speaks to us. It involves listening for His voice in scripture, prayer, and the world around us. As we cultivate this openness, we become more attuned to His guidance, leading to growth in our spiritual journey. Embracing this dynamic relationship allows us to experience the fullness of His presence and love. Through ongoing encounters, we discover new aspects of His character and deepen our understanding of His plans for our lives.

The continuous invitation from God to encounter Him is transformational, impacting every area of our lives. Each time we respond to His knock, we open ourselves to new dimensions of faith and understanding. This journey is not merely about personal growth; it is about becoming conduits of His love and grace to others. By accepting His invitation daily, we participate in a divine narrative that extends beyond ourselves. Ultimately, the\ongoing encounter with God is a journey that leads to profound transformation and purpose.

My Reflection:

____

____

____

Co-Pastor Cynthia Brown
Life In Victory International Ministries
5606 Marlboro Pike | District Heights, MD 20747
301-752-8672 (Cell)
301-568-LIFE (5433) Church
Lifeinvictory.org
Reaching, Reviving & Restoring Souls to the Kingdom

"..I am come that they might have life, and that they might have it more abundantly." John 10:10

www.ingramcontent.com/pod-product-compliance
Lightning Source LLC
LaVergne TN
LVHW010945110826
845149LV00013B/2767

* 9 7 9 8 9 9 2 6 9 0 2 8 6 *